Inside & Out

To Shikha

In the struggle for
the desirable

Jeremy Cronin
January 2003

Inside & Out

Poems from *Inside* and *Even the Dead* by
JEREMY CRONIN

DAVID PHILIP PUBLISHERS
Cape Town

First published 1999 by David Philip Publishers (Pty) Ltd, 208
Werdmuller Centre, Claremont 7708, Cape Town, South Africa

Inside was first published 1983 by Ravan Press and *Even The Dead*
1997 by David Philip Publishers and Mayibuye Books

ISBN 0-86486-401-9

Printed and bound by
Trident Press, Old Marine Drive, Cape Town 8001, South Africa

CONTENTS

Inside

Inside

POEM–SHRIKE

For a body I've rolled up
inventory item six two three: one pair
socks short prisoner's European, dealt
for a tail
a tight hand from a scuffed
awaiting-trial playing card pack and added
50 finest quality
Rizla gummed
cigarette blaadjies scorched black.
From a prison cell floor comes this barred
light of your back, your
beak was bent
uptight for a week, your call with its
inner-side scratch I've rasped, your eyes
sharpened on the grindstone
down in the prison workshop, then dipped
in an old Koo tin of water from which they emerge
dripping light
nail sharp, tense, each as an i-dot.
I check your
hungry parts
over again, longing by longing then
out
over the high walls I launch you now. . .

sshrike!

Overhead is mesh,
To one side the morgue,
To one side the gallows wing, this
Is our yard

Into which a raggedy
By happenstance
Butterfly has flown,

Fluttering
Halfway to panic
Halfway to give a damn

Springtime has come.
The years flow into each other.
The struggle goes on.

WALKING ON AIR

Prologue

In the prison workshop, also known as the seminar room;

In the seminar room, sawdust up the nose, feet in plane shavings, old jam tins on racks, a dropped plank, planks, a stack of mason's floats waiting assembly, Warder von Loggerenberg sitting in the corner;

In the prison workshop, also and otherwise named, where work is done by enforced dosage, between political discussion, theoretical discussion, tactical discussion, bemoaning of life without women, sawdust up the nose, while raging at bench 4, for a week long, a discussion raging above the hum of the exhaust fans, on how to distinguish the concept 'Productive' from the concept . . . 'Unproductive Labour';

In the prison workshop, then, over the months, over the screech of the grindstone, I'm asking John Matthews about his life and times, as I crank the handle, he's sharpening a plane blade, holding it up in the light to check on its bevel, dipping the blade to cool in a tin of water, then back to the grindstone, sparks fly: 'I work for myself' – he says – 'not for the boere';

In the prison workshop, with John Matthews making contraband goeters, boxes, ashtrays, smokkel salt cellars of, oh, delicate dovetailings;

Over the months, then, in the prison workshop, I'm asking John Matthews, while he works intently, he likes manual work, he likes the feel of woodgrain, he doesn't like talking too much, the making and fixing of things he likes, he likes, agh no, hayikona, slap-bang-bang, work for the jailers;

In the prison workshop, then, I ask John Matthews, was he present on the two days of Kliptown . . . 1955? . . . when the People's Congress adopted the Freedom Charter?

Actually

No he wasn't

He was there the day before, he built the platform

In the prison workshop, then, over the hum of exhaust fans,
between the knocking in of nails, the concept 'Productive', the
concept 'Unproductive Labour', feet in plane shavings, John Matthews
speaks by snatches, the making and fixing of things he likes,
though much, never, much you won't catch him speaking;

But here, pieced together, here from many months, from the prison
workshop

Here is one comrade's story.

* * *

Born to Bez Valley, Joburg
into the last of his jail term
stooped now he has grown

In this undernourished frame
that dates back
to those first years of his life.

He was nine
when his father came
blacklisted home

From the 1922
Rand Revolt,
and there with a makeshift

Forge in their backyard
a never again to be employed
father passed on to his son

A lifelong
love for the making
and fixing of things.

From Bez Valley it was,
veiled liked a bride in fine
mine-dump dust

He went out
to whom it may concern
comma

A dependable lad
comma
his spelling is good.

At fifteen he became
office boy at Katzenellenbogen's
cnr. von Wielligh

And President streets
where he earned £1 a week,
where he learned:

• Good spelling doesn't always count.
• The GPO telegram charge is reckoned per word.
• A word is 15 letters max.
• You have to drop ONE *l* from Katzenellenbogen Inc or
            HEAR ME BOY?! nex' time
        YOU'S gonna pay extra one word
                    charge your bliksem self.

And the recession came
but he got a bookkeeping job
with Kobe Silk

On the same block
        – John Edward
Matthews

Mondays to Fridays
on that same block
for 37 unbroken years until

The security police
picked him up . . . But first
way back to the thirties.

WEEKENDS IN THE THIRTIES:
church and picnics
by Zoo Lake

And later, deedle-deedle
– Dulcie, heel-toe
his future wife

Whom he courted with
(he can still do it)
diddle-diddle: the cake-walk

And always
on Sundays it was
church and church.

And then to Kobe Silk
there came
a new clerk

Myer Chames by name
a short little bugger who talked
Economics at lunch-break

And Myer Chames talked
of all hitherto existing societies,
the history of freeman

And slave, lord, serf,
guildmaster, journeyman,
bourgeois, proletarian and

In a word
John Matthews stopped
going to church.
His name got inscribed
inside

7

of a red party card.

He'd sell Inkululekos down by
Jeppestown
Friday nights

While the bourgeois press wrote
   RUSSIA HAS GONE SOFT ON HITLER
He learnt to fix duplicators and typewriters.

He was still selling
Inkululekos in 1943
When even the bourgeois press wrote

RED ARMY HAS BROKEN
BROKEN
THE BACK OF HITLER

In the year 1943 – born
to Dulcie and John
a daughter

Their first child
first of seven.
And now

Into the last months
of his 15 years
prison term

At nights in his cell
he peeps down at his face
in a mirror

In a mirror held low, about
belly-height,
wondering how he'll seem

To his grandchildren
from down there
next year when he comes out.

But that's later . . . back
to 1950
The Suppression of Communism Act

Membership becomes a punishable crime.
But laws only
postpone matters – somewhat.

There were still duplicators to fix
and typewriters to mend
through the 50s

Passive Resistance, the Congress Alliance,
    Defiance Campaign, Pass Burnings, Bus
    Boycott, Potato Boycott, the Women's
    March, the Treason Trial, the Freedom
    Charter, until

Until 1960: the massacre
        Sharpeville
        and Langa.

And people said: 'Enough,
        our patience, it has limits' . . . and so
it was no longer just typewriters and duplicators
                        to mend.

A man would come to the backyard and whisper:
                        30 ignitors
And John Matthews would make 30, to be
                        delivered to X.
And a man would come in the dead of night
These need storing comrade, some things
                wrapped in waterproof cloth.
        TERRORISTS BOMB POWERLINES
He would read in the bourgeois press, or
        MIDNIGHT PASS OFFICE BLAST
He'd sigh a small sigh
– Hadn't been sure
Those damned ignitors would work.

Finally.
1964.
After a quarter century in the struggle

A security police swoop
and John Matthews was one
among several detained.

White and 52
so they treated him nice.
They only made him stand

On two bricks
for three days
and three nights and

When he asked to go to the lavatory
they said:
                    Shit in your pants.

But the State needed witnesses
So they changed their tune.
Tried sweet-talking him round.
Think of your career
                    (that didn't work)
Think of the shame of going to jail
                    (that thought only
                    filled him with pride)
You really want kaffirs to rule?
                    (like you said)
Think of your wife
                    (Dulcie. Dulcie.
                    7 kids. Dulcie.
                    She's not political at all).

And there they had him.
On that score he was worried, it's true.
And they promised him freedom.
And they pressed him for weeks on end
Until finally he said:

Okay, agreed.

– But first I must speak with my wife.

Barely an hour it took them to find
and rush Dulcie Matthews
out to Pretoria Jail.

Then looking nice, because they let him shave, let him comb his
hair, looking nice then, chaperoned by smiling, matrimonial
policemen, shaven and combed, John Matthews got led out
to his wife, and holding her hand, they let him hold her hand,
he said

– Do you know why they've brought you?
And she said
– I do
And he said
– Dulcie I will never betray my comrades.
And with a frog in her throat she replied
– I'm behind you. One hundred percent.

So back they hauled John Matthews then and there,
back to the cells,
that was that, then, but
all the way down the passage
toe-heel, heel-toe, diddle-diddle
ONE HUNDRED PERCENT
I mean, he was high
Off the ground, man.

He was walking on air.

POLLSMOOR SKETCHES

I

It's never too late
For tattooed tears
Trane implies
With purple tear-drops
That stream down his cheek

Skin deep.

II

Las' time I getta ten years
But ony I pusha fife.
You wants to know why?
Ees because I no shtupid.
For eenstance, I polishing in da boeb
Deesa peeg, he come, he shtand over me
He say: 'Hey Portugoose,
Why you no polisha clean?'
                    I theenk:
FUCKA YOU!
                    (I say
nothingk.)

III

The pay's kak
The prisoners give bek
And today my name's
AAAAAAAAgterhek!
AAAAAAAAgterhek!
That's me
Ting ting fok kak bek
I'm a turnkey.

IV

I'll shoot down Vorster any day of the week.
Hey kommie, you get me a gat
And I'll get you a boer
You bleddy cocksucking, kaffir loving,
Communis jew, I'll donner you up,

So pally, in your golden chains of friendship
Will you count me as a link?
So bra, will you see me right?
Jail's a shit sandwich
And every day we get a bite.

V
Listen man, I'm in boeb
For something
I hardly didn't do.

Course I knew Bram Fischer.
He tune me one day straight:
       – Pssssssss
           Hulloa Ginger.

VI
'. . .in this epic theatre the actor does everything to make himself per-
ceived standing between the audience and the event he portrays. . .'
                                                 – Brecht

  Kom, kom, kom, kom, kom, kom, you donders,
    Stand two-two, two-two, two-two!
For a head count and thumpprint check.
  – Johannes Stephanus Februarie!
Gives a small stylized skip.
  – Ja, o.b.
(Ou baas worn short with long use)

And begins his casual sideways shuffle, in caricature of haste.
He rolls exaggerated thumbs in ink,
And with all the care of Albrecht Dürer
Prints them, tenderly.
In his hair he wipes off ink
As he slips back with head bowed and
Panache to his place in line.

There is,
Between Johannes Stephanus Februarie
And submission,
This epic gap.

MOTHO KE MOTHO KA BATHO BABANG
(A PERSON IS A PERSON BECAUSE OF OTHER PEOPLE)

By holding my mirror out of the window I see
Clear to the end of the passage
There's a person down there.
A prisoner polishing a doorhandle.
In the mirror I see him see
My face in the mirror,
I see the fingertips of his free hand
Bunch together, as if to make
An object the size of a badge
Which travels up to his forehead
The place of an imaginary cap.
        (This means: *A warder.*)
Two fingers are extended in a vee
And wiggle like two antennae.
        (He's being watched.)
A finger of his free hand makes a watch-hand's arc
On the wrist of his polishing arm without
Disrupting the slow-slow rhythm of his work.
        (*Later.* Maybe, later we can speak.)
Hey! Wat maak jy daar?
        – a voice from around the corner.
No. Just polishing baas.
He turns his back to me, now watch
His free hand, the talkative one,
Slips quietly behind
        – *Strength brother*, it says,
In my mirror,
        A black fist.

THINKS . . .

Fish yes, not flesh nor fowl
here in this woolless world

Of the public aquarium's many
after hours, see

Off the top of my head
a stream of bubbles

That rises, that billows
above me, inside it

Is written:
THINKS dot-dot-dot

And no
word of a lie

Here in the tanks
of the public aquarium's

Filter green
iridescent mineral waters

Where always the time
seems like after hours

Where the looks of the guards
have surely departed

Leaving on glass
dot-dot-dot

Just
the prints of their stump-noses.

GROUP PHOTO FROM PRETORIA LOCAL ON THE OCCASION OF A FOURTH ANNIVERSARY (NEVER TAKEN)

An uprooted tree leaves
 behind it a hole in the ground
But after a few months
You would have to have known
 that something grew here once.
And a person's uprooted?
Leaves a gap too, I suppose, but then
 after some years. . .
There we are
 seated in a circle,
Mostly in short pants, some of us barefoot,
Around the spot where four years before
When South African troops were repulsed before Luanda

Our fig tree got chopped
 down in reprisal. – That's Raymond
Nudging me, he's pointing
At Dave K who looks bemusedly
Up at the camera. Denis sits on an upturned
Paraffin tin. When this shot was taken
He must have completed
 17 years of his first
Life sentence.
 David R at the back is saying
Something to John, who looks at Tony who
Jerks his hand
 So it's partly blurred.
There we are, seven of us
 (but why the grinning?)
Seven of us, seated in a circle,
The unoccupied place in the centre
 stands for what happened
Way outside the frame of this photo.
So SMILE now, hold still and
 click
  I name it: Luanda.
For sure an uprooted tree

leaves behind a hole in the ground.
After a few years
You would have to have known
    it was here once. And a person?
There we are
    seated in our circle, grinning,
    mostly in short pants,
    some of us barefoot.

4 times 12
first thing in the morning is 48
. . . 48, I think what Engels said
about freedom being
the understanding of necessity
take away 6 is
. . . 42 more weeks, what'm I saying? MONTHS!
                    I want to shout
                    up into my mirror
from today I've only got
exactly
42 MORE MONTHS!
                    But you know
along this corridor we live
only in some ways
according to the same time
when we count other people's victories for instance
as our own (which they are).
                    But there're those other times
parcelled
in separate
brown paper packets.
A time that walks in circles.
A time that flattens itself
incredibly thin
                    disappears
into the backs of mirrors
or drips from the taps.
When I first came to jail
some of my comrades had served
thirteen years –
drop by drop, they've been inside now
since before the armed struggles
in Mozambique and Zimbabwe
had even begun.
                    I lie in bed
picturing myself
stepping out
in a new set of clothes
with a brown paper packet
– letters

seven years of letters
under my arm
            – in 42 months' time
when some of these comrades
            (counting
            Mozambique, Angola, Zimbabwe,
            . . . perhaps Namibia by then)
                        might
STILL be inside.

FOR COMRADES IN SOLITARY CONFINEMENT

Every time they cage a bird
the sky shrinks. A little.

Where without appetite –
you commune
with the stale bread of yourself,
pacing to and fro, to shun,
one driven step on ahead
of the conversationist
who lurks in your head.
You are an eyeball
you are many eyes
hauled to high windows
to glimpse, dopplered by mesh
how-how-how long?
the visible, invisible, visible
across the sky
the question mark – one
sole ibis flies.

DEATH ROW

I
The first we hear is this tremendous
        cajoling laughter.

Ten minutes later, above our cells
Squeak-squeak-squeak, across the catwalk
Walks an unfamiliar warder.

It's three fokken terrorists – he says,
Not grasping, yet.

Who we are.
They're impossible man. A person
Can't do
Nothing with them.

Johannes Shabangu.
David Moise.
Bobby Tsotsobe.

                        Having
Skipped the country
        trained in diverse parts
                slipped back clandestinely
Dug
        diggers of the earth
                residers of holes underground.
Sons of the soil
        breath to be swallowed
                breath swallowed by the night
In the night
        darker than plain dark
                and all so quiet
Sappers
        Soweto's sons
                stalkers
                        Who blew up
Sasol 2 by Secunda

Uncle Tom's Hall
        Booysens, the cop shop
Dube line
        likewise a place near
                Malelane
                                Caught
Caught in a shoot-out
        captured at Matola
                strung upside down
Probed without days
        in a night
                in a river of needles
The clammy hood
        choke hold
                a year without season
For months
        your bodies probed
                months long until

                        finally you were led
                unbowed into court
                        and charged
                all three
                        with high treason.

Now nine months already, brothers
You've been sitting
On death row.

II
What concerning C section
can I tell you?

What down here could be different
from B section?

A section? Or from wherever
it is inside this slaughterhouse
they've just randomly
shifted you from?

Listen . . . two walls to the left.
A garden – I think,
from where this sound
leaks in.
A guinea-hen's call – we've been told,
glass on glass
a pocketful of marbles weeping
deep in her throat, but don't ask

On Wednesday mornings
almost every other week,
another, staggered sound
like bioscope seats flapped
back. What's that!? Don't

        Ask me, brothers, I

        . . . Perhaps I didn't hear.

III
Of course we never get to speak,
As such, to each other.
We're still fifty yards, one corridor,
Many locked locks apart.

Nkosi sikelel', we try singing, at night.
Us down here, to you,
Three condemneds, along there.

Morena . . . we whiteys sing,
Mayibuye iAfrika, and muffled
Far-off chortling, you guys
Call back: *Encore! Encore!*

IV
Then it's you singing slow
Antiphonal phrases,
Three tongues floating over
      That audible
Drop which gathers,
The words thrumming in your

23

Throats, brothers,
About which
Some Wednesday morning
Three nooses will go.

One voice leading:
Arrraaise ye, high up,
Everynight,
Deeper, two in the chorus:
Prisoners from your slumbers
Called and
To boil or
Respond like a
Ripple like a
Lurch like a
Ukuhlabelela
is to
Glow like a
Growl like a
Glow like a
Boil like a
Bean stew like a
Ripple like a
Bus queue weaves like a
Moves like a
Stalks like a
Moves like a
Fighter
Ukuhlabelela
Three voices
Called or
Moise
Combine or responding
Tsotsobe
Weaving
Shabangu
In and
Voices
Each other
Around of, sliding
Into each night's

Finale, all three
Three now
As one: *Tha-a-a*
Inta
nasha – na – ale
yoonites tha
hooman
reissss. A-MAAA
– ndla ! longleev
sisulu-mandela-tambo
LONGleev! LONGleev!
          shouted longleev!
Your voices, brothers
Down these concrete
Corridors of power.

The Naval Base

I

I close my eyes, and it's the sea's
entering soft foot, through
97 98 99 one
HUNdred! And call COMing!
across the streamlet
with its wild cat prints
through the port jackson scrub,
I check the beach, the old jetty,
and now into the house:
the wardrobe, pantry, under the beds.
These all being the finite number
of places a five-year-old
kid would hide, nose pinched
to stop his sneeze – the point
being not to be found
too soon,
nor ever to hide
where you wouldn't hear
my feet closing in, despite the precautions
stepped up in these last few years,
as my feet approach, I could say:
I have come
just to troll
for mackerel from the pier's end, but who
would believe that
now? With you
in there, your nose pinched
hidden in the deepest ignorance
of the bulldozers moving on the zinc camp,
of the trek fishermen group area'd
out for the submarine pens,
as my feet approach, something
moves with the sea's snuffling
in through the countless fish
tastes of its underwater salads, awash
in the half-forgotten house by the beach
amongst the feeders, its stone valves,
these almost empty rooms,
shell, scale, pelt,

in the armed white camp, behind
the newest precautions, and my feet
approaching w-a-r-m-e-r. Feet
stumbling in this undergrowth.
Me hiding in there, ears pricked up.
Me out here circling about. There is
between the two of us, in this
necessary space, nothing,
nothing that could be learned,
or forgotten now
by backing off.

II

Like Jonah I recall the darkness.
At ritual and appointed hours,
in cod liver oil my tongue
would be anointed.
A symbol weighed inside my head
An anchor fixed betwixt my legs.
Eaten, then excreted, these
my imagined rites of passage – Yes,
childhood weighs
an anchor in my head, like an unanswered question
bucking to start into the tide's
smack in a hundred off-beat
digressions the snoek boats gasp
uh! – uh! – uh!– uh! – throttling
at first light, at sixty
glottal stops the minute – Where?
Where do babies come from?

I ask a sea anemone.
It folds a secret
mouth in its mouth.
People get married – says my mother.
When you're older you'll learn – says my father.
And the snoek boats go
uh! – uh! – uh! – uh! – uh!
Through a world charged with half hints
warmed with buckscent and
the wildest pelargonium, the mountain puts
a tentative toe in the sea.
In mid-bay a sea proffers
two dozing nostrils and
one laconic flipper. Where
do babies come from?

In winter the rains wash down
tennis balls from the coloured quarters on the hill.
I'd find them, Moses-like
in our streamlet's reeds.
Under my jersey I place them,

snuggled to my belly, in winter
when I'd whisper
into Jenny Brown's brown ear.
– *You STUPID!* She says.
Jenny Brown my parents' maid
– *Only women can make lighties.*
                    – she laughs.

III

I cannot disclaim that string-thin, five-year old boy
with big ears and bucked teeth from thumbsucking late,
who woke to dockyard hooters on mornings of mackerel-green sea
that cast up sea-eggs, argonauts, unexplained white rubber
                                                    balloons.
A soft sea full of cutting things, of sharkstooth, barnacles, and
                                                    ultra marines.
Who polished with envy and Silvo his pa's ceremonial sword.
Who dreamt of mama and the ocean's lap-lap,
and that one day the tide would ride out,
yes ride oh right out, uncovering bedclothes.
That boy, that endless earache, who knew at five,
because he learnt by heart, the naval salute, the sign of the cross,
the servant's proper place, and our father who art.
– This five-year old boy,
this shadow, this thing stuck to my feet.

IV

Anointed. Let my nose be now attentive.
Anointed, the waters of that sky,
The fish oil factory, and the acre
Just beyond.

Anointed is the wind that slicks back
And smooths down forever
The wavelets of the bay

Where the gun carriage rattled,
And the slow march marched,
Where lowered was a widow into widowhood,
And the blank shots got fired
Blankly into air.

Let my nose be now attentive,
From the morning watch,
Even until night, from the first dockyard hooter

From the depths crying out, this dissolution in the wind,
Water, fish, oil, factory, and
The burial acre just beyond.

V
I wasn't allowed to be present when
delirious with pain he said
(I was told many times after)
– *Jeremy must play cricket,* spoken three times,
three times over, while his body writhed and wasted.

Thus my father passed on
his patrimony of aspiration.

He was thirty-four when he died.

During the war he'd sailed on convoys to Murmansk and
                                                    Archangel,
– slender evidence this, against all else, as I search now
for retrospective conciliation, perhaps
because to this day his last inconsequences
still voyage up through his pain,
all night zig-zag in my torpedoed dreams stumps fly.

Venture to the Interior

PROLOGUE

Now in your cockpit
from your pilot's seat within
test the distant parts of this machine.
Take the tongue-tip and feel up
t-t-t-t-t
there, just
behind your upper front teeth
the ribbed shoal that runs back and up
to a solid arch of bone.
Beyond, slide along the soft velum's central crease
peeling back on your tongue's joy stick
until you touch
the stem from which depends
a strange
perhaps forbidden fruit aaaaah!
say aaaaah!
working the throttles of your glottis.
And now
to cool a while
let the tongue untwine
returning to its berth.
Let lip touch lip
hmmmmm, mmmmm.
Flick the switch to In
then Out: these
being the two prevailing winds.

Are all systems go?
– Good.
Then let flesh be made words.

CAVE-SITE

        I want you
to prise carefully
sound
        from sound
to honour by speaking
(and sometimes to discard)
to lift, cough,
        breccia, rock, sediment
layer through layer
                        in this
mouth or
        cave-site of word
root, birdbone,
        shells of meaning
left in our mouths
by thousands of years of
        human occupation.

LITANY

Out of the primal swamps
down the line of the mudfish
through the snake where your ways parted
after the hardening of the palate
you came
        to me o
            Amphibian Rose
tchareep grrrtch-grrrtch
            tchareeep tchareeep tchareeep
            Protrusible Shadow
            Tree of Tastebuds
kree-kree-kree-kree
        sssszzz
            from this jungle of unmapped sounds
        you arise
            Elastic Denizen
            Abettor of Mastication
            Disporting Porpoise
            Friend to Deglutition
            Concavity turned Turtle
sszzzzzzzzzzzz(_____!)
            Convexity of Muscle
        you come
            whirra – whirra – whirrra – whirrra
                        dove
            Love Scout
            Periscope of Pleasure
            Winged Breath
                    you come
                        bearing the leaves of speech
        Tongue!
O Ark of Language.

PLATO'S CAVE

. . . would they not assume that the shadows they saw were real things?

Imagine a chamber that's cave-like and runs
down and down underground,
and imagine
within this chamber
there are prisoners with strange anatomical names.
Each is fastened here or there
and enfolded in dark.

Suppose further that these prisoners are restless,
that they hoist the back of their tongue
to enclose a pocket of air, and then
with a quick downward stroke they make
                    !quagga!
painting a palatal click on the roof of their cave.

Or suppose, hearing snatches of news,
they are filled with deep longing,
these prisoners who incessantly mimic
the sounds of their land
down in the blue-veined stopes
down in the very confines of their chamber.

Supposing all this,
do you think they'd assume
this shadow play was real?
That these prisoners could forget
the struggles of their brothers and sisters
there outside where these sounds
bathed in the daylight, may

someday, grow into words?

LABYRINTH I

from a blanket
– unpicked,
twined for strength,
balled for concealment,
taken out in the dead of night,
this cotton thread,
weighted with a comb
on its casting end, this
– is a cable.

Blind guessing
on distance and angle,
the comb skating off
many times
from under the chink, tentative,
of my locked door, trailing
its cotton tail, lifeline
out, as it jigs
back at last to rebound
under my neighbour's
cell door, this
– is a cable.

a thread of contact
down which to pass
a meagre
well read, smuggled-in, month-old, scrap of
– newspaper.

Our land holds its hard
Wooden truths like a peach
A pip:
            Out at Athlone
By the power station
Over the two cooling towers, the wind
Turns visible in its spoors.
Skin and bone, zig zag,
Through the khaki bush
It hums, the wind tongues
Its gom-gom, frets a gorah,
In a gwarrie bush the wind,
So I fancy, mourns, thin
Thin with worries:
            Goringhaicona
Goringhaiqua Gorachouqua: sounds
Like at the back of our sky
Cicadas' songs ache: Hessequa
Hacumqua, like vocables swallowed
In frogs' throats: Cochoqua,
The names of decimated
Khoikhoin tribes – their cattle stolen,
Lands seized
As their warriors died
Charging zig-zag into musket fire,
Those warriors who've left behind
Their fallen spears that our land
Like a peach its pip
            Holds now:

This unfinished task.

If you're asking: whose land?
Under the pounding of wood, consider
Between the grinding conversations, stone to stone,
Where the sun gives up its vegetable holds,
How many centuries
Have been stirred into putu?

Whose land? – if you're wondering
It's no use telephoning: Stamp the earth
Ask among the bones
Where the frogs bring down
Rain on their own heads, and the earth
Chews, chews,
Like a pair of scissors never getting fat.

Grain's seed, grass, shrub's roots
Where the men's bones with their snuff pouches,
Women's bones with their porridge sticks, ask
There where lineage on lineage sits
Tucked in this earth.

KARROO I

Under this spreadeagled
sky, in flight a tickbird,
neck tucked up, looks
bronchitic; a lizard
gathers breath; stone lies on stone,
and the road, a chewed thong
through this buckhide,
breathless unscrunched land
so parched, words,
of birth difficult,
stick, agh, buck, kop, grab,
shrub, rock, klip,
stick, traveller, in the back of your throat.

With each generation, you said,
The entire race passes
Through the body of its womanhood
                                        – Olive Schreiner

along these Karroo tracks
dissecting truths
about men, God,
. . . women,
your plaits pinned up,
              chewing
on pieces of paper, and later
in London
you looked
into a microscope
at spermatozoa, looked
back to twelve flat stones
          O God consume my offering.
          O God, like Elijah to be licked
                    up in a heavenly fire.

          O God, this little thing so much desired.
And God was unmoved.
For was it not, fiction aside,

a little girl and a lamb chop
left uneaten?
Its fat, like spent seed
trickling down the side of a stone
beneath this African, this spreadeagled sun.
     – O Olive Schreiner
      ceaseless campaigner
against all oppressors,
jingoes, warmongers,
God, Rhodes, the British South Africa Company.
Sowing seeds, letters to meetings,
you were too unwell to attend:

I am glad
    To hear of your meeting
I am glad that in your meeting
    Men and Women are combined
    Because men and women
    Are the right and left sides of humanity.
I am especially glad that women workers are taking
their place in this meeting
    As the most poorly paid
    Heavily pressed section of labour
    It is necessary women workers
    Should learn solidly to combine.
I hope your meeting
    Will be large and successful – signed:
        Olive Schreiner, your letters

    still keep arriving.

KARROO II

Into some hypothetical hotel – The Grand,
or The Milner – night sifts through
your words, and an opened window.
From generation to generation
language trekking on
through each of our throats:
koppie, sheepkraal, koppie,
milkbush, the town location, this whole
spanned outscattering dusted
in moon track,
farmhouse, prickly pears,
the star leaking sky, touched
all with your improbable word: *ethereal.*

      Lonely, lonely, lonely,
somewhere out there deep, Olive Schreiner,
into this night,
in a broken down shack
(not knowing
she'll stir the world yet)
is this small intense girl,
deep in her book,
black as the night:
your great-great granddaughter.

THE IVORY TRAIL

Along this wheel scar, down the Ivory Trail,
Behind my canines, in the dust of my throat
You can hear my ancestor,
The Great White Hunter:
  'Three thousand', he would growl,
  'and some two hundred and fifty odd,
  back in 1918, yep,
    my best year, grandson – a drought.'
He nods. Hawks. Gobs.
  – Black Ivory,
That's what he called
  The contract mine labour he recruited north of the latitude
  22 degrees south.
  My forebear who went
Renaming the sons of man,
For unless a man be born again
  Sockies, Sikkies, Fife, Fifteen, Knife,
  Gladstone, Wellington, Houtkop, Jim,
  Tickey, Flappies, Doek . . .
Into those ultra-deep levels,
More than a mile below the surface of the earth,
Contracted into low-roofed
Chambers where they move
A quarter million tons of rock
In a single stope each month,
While the pressure like a smothered
Shout, builds and buckles
While the stress points
Shift until, as they say,

She bumps . . .
Tread
Tread, tread ever so softly now, grandpa,
There's men down there,
From 1918, remember? – and still
Chewing earth.

THE RIVER THAT FLOWS THROUGH OUR LAND

A swift stream in the high mountains, dropping dental, lateral
Clicking in its palate like the flaking of stone tools;
And a wide river that grazes the plains,
Lows like the wind in summer maize.
And a waterfall that hums through a turbine
And is whirled into light.

A river that carries many tongues in its mouth.

And a river that flows from times of peace,
And times of war when its fords became slippery,
A river that has bathed spears and bridal parties.

And a river that trickles
Down the worker's face.
The salt river that welds tomorrow forward,
Steel girder on girder and concrete.

This is the river that flows through this land.

To learn how to speak
With the voices of the land,
To parse the speech in its rivers,
To catch in the inarticulate grunt,
Stammer, call, cry, babble, tongue's knot
A sense of the stoneness of these stones
From which all words are cut.
To trace with the tongue wagon-trails
Saying the suffix of their aches in -kuil, -pan, -fontein,
In watery names that confirm
The dryness of their ways.
To visit the places of occlusion, or the lick
In a vlei-bank dawn.
To bury my mouth in the pit of your arm,
In that planetarium,
Pectoral beginning to the nub of time
Down there close to the water-table, to feel
The full moon as it drums
At the back of my throat
Its cow-skinned vowel.
To write a poem with words like:
I'm telling you,
Stompie, stickfast, golovan,
Songololo, just boombang, just
To understand the least inflections,
To voice without swallowing
Syllables born in tin shacks, or catch
The 5.15 ikwata bust fife
Chwannisberg train, to reach
The low chant of the mine gang's
Mineral glow of our people's unbreakable resolve.

To learn how to speak
With the voices of this land.

Some Uncertain Wires

GRANPA KEMP

A flash of tarred wattle poles in the corners of the eyes,
the only apparent movement through these dried flats from
the road.
Strange that wide spaces could have made
such a narrow mind – this is Granpa Kemp country,
and those, he would have said, are his poles.

Retired to a smallholding, mealie patch, chicken hok,
and a garage filled with used Firestone tyres,
he was guided, when I knew him, still by those self-taught
headstrong maxims, and a spike in the pantry for the bills.

Foreman of a polegang he had been
when they worked with post office cables to stretch
and peg out this land; he bothered to speak
a few bastardized words of Xhosa – for command,
while every new pole carried
the pulse of colonialism in its overhead wires.

Most of a lifetime he gave, lonely out there
as the loneliest pole they ever raised.
In the end his eyes were dried to pale blue,
glass caps, insulators on a cross-beam.

GRANMA KEMP

An electric device listens in my cell's walls –
it must have been a bit like this you felt
with those, what you called,
creepy crawlies, and the big sun besides.

To Humansdorp, brought back from the Great War
along with his unextracted shrapnel, you were
The English Bride.

Forty years on, still pale and transplanted, my Granma Violet,
late afternoons I'd wait with a small boy's fascination
until, parasoled, behatted, watering-can in hand
carefully you'd tread, down kitchen steps
into Africa

My grandma had been getting old, of course,
so my mother felt she should perhaps
some time pay the call
she'd been putting off for years.

Her telegram read:
ARRIVING THURSDAY NEXT STOP SHORT VISIT
It was wired from Cape Town through to Humansdorp.

Four hours later, the sudden appearance of this message made
my poor grandma's dicky heart stop
dead.

The ceremony was held over until Thursday next,
and of course, etc., in short
nothing more was said.

But oh yes, I remember those telegraph wires!

When I was five we made a trip to my grandparents once
– both were still alive.
I didn't ask my mother then
had these place-names
(when she'd travelled away from her childhood
– but going the other way)
each marked just another hundred more miles
thankfully erased?

Listen between Cape Town
past shanty towns, up to the Boland,
over dried flats, the roadsigns, the Riviersonderend,
to those thin telegraph wires.

Do they still hum? Is it still liar, liar, liar, your nose
is as long as something beginning I spied
with my little eye riddled with too much road,
birdsperch that hums its quavering song: Ai,
Ai, the witbors kraai flies from here to Mosselbaai, George,
Outeniqua, Tsitsikamma, Storms River gorge – this nostalgia
is thicker than water, my family,
between generations, is all space
half filled with childhood rhymes, joined
by some uncertain wires

Love Poems

INVOKING MY MUSE

Suppose these lines
Were to try for her grin, being
Slightly ironic yet
Altogether serious, if you see
What I mean?

Suppose the dark times, of unmarked cars,
Of our half expecting an unwanted
Knock on the door.
Suppose
A room which I enter and something is hurriedly
Shuffled away . . .

A pamphlet? An illegal pamphlet?
It might be because

I would like these lines to invoke
Suddenly from out of those times
With a certain facial expression
One eye closed to modulate the glare,
Her head sideways tilted, mouth wry,
The back of her forearm sweeps
Wisps away from her brow . . .

To be remembered in all this?

Partly, the light I've switched on, and
Partly: (SHIT MAN Jeremy, I almost thought you . . .)

Her grin.

Itchy with its
sound of crickets
this night could be
    anywhere (almost)

    – But it isn't.

As the first watch warder
arrives in our passage

Two remote controlled doors opened
and clanged shut

Three manually operated grilles opened
and clanged shut

Five locks
    just the beginning
of what lies between us.

But my love
to be removed
jailed endorsed out banished
man from woman is

After all
nothing unusual in this

Our country, in these times
in this night full of crickets
when to say plainly:

    'I love you'
is also
a small act
of solidarity with all the others.

Tonight is an envelope
Into which I climb, sliding between its folds
The letter I, flesh made paper
Turning in half, then again
        sleeplessly over.
Never more than 500 words
One letter per month quota, I take
Three weeks at least to arrive.
After their reckoning of words, after the censors,
After the ink-check, code-check, comes
A rubber stamping.
Tonight is this envelope into which I slide
As the selfsame letter formed on my tongue
My tongue turned into paper – tonight perhaps
Taking off as no more than 500 words
In a bat of the lids, it's just
Possible to consider me as flying at last
As three week old words, behind the inside flap's
        Gummed
Touch to reach you.

A PRAYER IN SEARCH OF BEADS

As a child I learned
to follow blind the circular path
where the hand was guide to the tongue
each bead unlocked
its own particular prayer.

But now I have to hope
for some reverse palpability to emerge.
I close my eyes – fervently,
Un zip . . . *Un zip* I intone
fumbling with its sounds
as if I hoped to touch
in that word, bump, bump,
the tingling, the warm
rosary down your spine.

Faraway city, there
with salt in its stones,
under its windswept doek,

There in our Cape Town where
they're smashing down homes
of the hungry, labouring people
– will you wait for me, my love?

In that most beautiful,
desolate city of my heart
where if staying on were passive
life wouldn't be what it is.

Not least for those rebuilding
yet again their demolished homes
with bits of plastic, port jackson saplings,
anything to hand – unshakeably

Defiant, frightened, broken,
and unbreakable are the people of our city.

– Will you wait for me, my love?

LABYRINTH II

... and Ariadne, her beautiful erotic thread unwinding, guiding
him in the stone darkness ... (Yannis Ritsos)

I'm unravelled by day, at night
I weave now and weave
with the fading scent
of soap, following its thread down
to another time, another bed
to where a-hooked and kicking we
ssshh – wildeye, like
two katonkel, made love.

Or awoke, a-tangled
androgyn, twice-fourlegged:
– us and the bed.
Laden with scents of voyages made
of voyages still to become
its pine frame solid enough to take
a mattress of foam, being
not too wide, being
              – just so.

It had sheets that knew creases,
a pillow once swollen,
in daytime it became
a settee, where the back
of a knitting needle purled
at my upper left arm
as you knit and knit
the far end of this twine.

as I remember
these things are ribbed:
    a sanddune
untouched:
    a fishing boat
on a slipway:
    the roof
of your mouth.

CHAPMAN'S PEAK

The sea's break
from high up's a continuous shush . . .

She's a wingbone.
Not the Atlantic,

Nor the Atlantic's
duffling fog up on a headland.

Stone. Nor ligament
of stone fibre. She's

not the wide
fall, the gulled float, the wheel, plunge

and squinny, or the wind's
persiflage where it goes

down to the wheeze and
scuttle by the seafringe. But

a wingbone. The deft
birdpoise in her hip.

VISITING ROOM

To admit light,
that's a window's vocation,
or a man to a wife
at this very place
where the wall becomes
for the briefest moments – a window,
shadowed by warders.
A glass plate, its sheer
quiddity, its coldness

forever between our hands.

A LOVE POEM

I write: She's like some unnamed succulent of the veld.
    She says: That's really flat.
But I'm trying to say it like I feel.
    Then you'd better think twice, she insists.

So I write:
    Skimming two dark pools, her eyes,
    her eyelashes are glistening dragonflies.

That's better, she says, but
Why all this delicate nature stuff? It wasn't
A flower that taught you how to drive.

I SAW YOUR MOTHER

I saw your mother
with two guards
through a glass plate
for one quarter hour
on the day that you died.

'Extra visit, special favour'
I was told, and warned
'The visit will be stopped
if politics is discussed.
Verstaan – understand!?'
on the day that you died.

I couldn't place
my arm around her,
around your mother
when she sobbed.

Fifteen minutes up
I was led
back to the workshop.
Your death, my wife,
one crime they managed
not to perpetrate
on the day that you died.

YOUR DEEP HAIR

Remember the mierkat's
footfall down the inner-sleeve of night,
under the milkbush, under the curdled
star clouds of galactic semen
spilled across the sky, you turned in sleep and
from your deep hair tumbled
aromatic buchu and the wide veld.

Three months now.
Scalp shaved,
you died, they say,
your head encased in wraps.

EYELIDS

They signalled quietly,
two flags of their own.
Down for refusal. Up in surprise.
Down again for laughter – each
eyelid was restless as five
workmen or a broom, all
touch and go, they'd stroke
along the surface of an eyeball.
As careful as
a teaspoon of light,
a pinch of salt, or a dark petticoat.
Who can forget how they'd unveil
– between blinks,
         through all tears –
an unbreakable strength.

A bay scooped in Cape mountains
down a hillside of vygies, and namaqualand
daisies, and a wooden bungalow that holds nights of candles.
In alliekreukels are those eyes, a voice
indistinguishable from the dark cleft
where the freshwater spring sings arums and watercress.
Listen to the breathing that moves
through the anchored kelp beds. Look
the duiker's low flight to Bellows Rock.
That is also her gaze. Many times.
And if you're there, read
in the margins of the tidewash, in the sandpiper's prints
a lesson inscribed in forgetting – it is not.

Somewhere inside here
Like part of me still deeply alive
Behind the blocked orifices of a head cold
While out there everything merged
Into its winter
Into its smudge and Claremont's nose dripped . . .
Drips on a window-pane
Named for a cosmonaut, Valentina the cat
Still orbits in her sleep
Before the electric heater's yellow coil
Yellow the straw mat
And a drying pair of tights
                    Tossed
Quick over the back of a chair . . .

I still go there, I mean
A small room
Behind my eyebrows
                    – Out of the rain

MIRROR

Hold my hand and step
into the mirror
between the cool perimeters
of its drowned amphitheatre, wade in
bellyheight . . . shoulder height . . . point blank
snorkel down to the past
below the waterbug that crinkles
the meniscus of time.
Swim behind these curtains of exhalation to where suspended
our submerged years
hang like dark bamboos
their feet shackled to the water-bed
their heads
still recall the sun.

Now hold tight
as we swim back to the air, but always
. . . only your face stares out with its nose
pressed
against an impassable glass frontier.

Isiququmadevu

ISIQUQUMADEVU

Take care, it's said, lest your shadow
    crosses the deepest of pools.

You think
    that's only old superstitions?

You won't accept
    that pools in South Africa are swallowers.

Gigantic swallowers into which
    not only the heedless may plunge.

Here where a thin sky
    plummets through the catwalk

Between bars and mesh and
    into the tunnels of my eyeballs

Until with a nerve
    sprung faraway splash the sky lands

Blue. When I first came to prison
    I'd write about rivers

Now my poems
    are all about pools,

Pools and mirrors into which
    I've been slipping it seems

Into that retrograde self
    where imaginary maidens

Come down to bathe
    where the old pronoun,

I, the swimmer behind eyelids,
    Isiququmadevu dreams

Daylong . . . agh, of
    snatching their clothes.

WHITE FACE, BLACK MASK

Thoughts
    concerning the person
    named Who:
Who is naked beneath his clothes,
Who is black in the night,
Who is
    unwashed before his bath,
and you mustn't suck cents
    you never know
Who might have touched them last.
Who is mask.
Who is beyond
    mask, lock, yale, bolt, chain, electric alarm.
Who,
    son of Who,
Who's Who, when the dog barks
there also is Who.
Who peeps through windows.
Who desires my mother, without a pass.
Who wields
    a double-edged knife.
Who entertains
    my darkest
desires.
Who,
    a temporary permanent
sojourner in my dream's backyard.
Who walks through our night.
Who stalks our women.
Who looks at my sister
    with longing.
        Yes,
Who.

I run a length of cotton twine between my teeth
Or I consider the hedging reticent tentative forward motion
                                        of an ant
        With its two blind man's sticks
        Tock-tock tock-tock
        Feeling left and right
I feel like being in love – but with whom?
It's six o'clock I'm writing these words
About stretches of bare concrete that cast me
Into the infinity of small things
I've begun to observe most closely a spider in the corner of
                                        my cell
You'd think in prison I'd empathise only with the ant
Trussed head and foot now in a web – but it's also the spider
The spider, this intense alliance eight legs to a bobbin – consider
How it swings on its toothedge how it trawls in the currents
At six o'clock as I spin out
The interminable lines of a love poem to no-one
        Tock-tock tock-tock
To no-one in particular – and now
As if at the edge of my poem

I sit
        And I wait.

A grounded parachutist, he pulls the ripcord
of his pyjama pants, he hums
he's got the whole wide world in his hand.
he thinks of Ryle's distinction:
knowing how/knowing that.
In magazines
are lips that slide from 2-D faces
to fly towards his metal supper plate.

They find it difficult to think
in three dimensions – he hears
the radio say for explanation
why there're so few SA engineers
who're black – Jesus!
Lock a white boy up
a few years inside, you'll find him
knowing that/but not knowing
how there're three dimensions to a woman.

Removed from the city now I live
an exile from confirmation
in a thousand reflective plate-glass fronts,
in ten thousand human faces, out of habitat
I've shrunk.
But how once I moved on escalators!
City, I lived your vibrance once,
I, multiplicand, you the power of ten.
Yet not yet beyond division, both,
simple and long.

Poet, I too have tasted the city,
your polyglot, cosmopolite, mankind city!
On escalators I have felt the thrum simultaneous
I was ascending, that one descending,
that person also was me.
Yet Walt Whitman this unity is not yet won.
Our essence the aggregate of social relations, I live divided
from my city: my city
not yet
        diversely one

A STEP AWAY FROM THEM

There's a poem called that
by Frank O'Hara, the American,
it begins: *It's my lunch hour so I go*
for a walk . . . I like the poem, sometime
I'll write it out complete, but just for now
I've got this OK Bazaars plastic packet
in my left hand, and my right
hand's in my pocket (out of sight),
how else to walk lunch hour
summertime Cape Town with
one gloved hand? And now
I'm going past The Cape Clog
– Takeaways, it says it's
The Home of The Original
ham 'n cheese – Dutch Burgers,
past the unsegregated toilets on
Greenmarket Square. A cop van's
at the corner. On a bench
3 black building workers eat
from a can of Lucky
Star pilchards. They're
in various shapes and sizes. It's a fact.
Though you'd think
post boxes'd be all
just one size. I'm sweating a bit,
heart pumps, mouth dry, umm
Gone one, I say slipping
past the Groote Kerk when
an Iranian naval sailor asks
What's the time? IRANIAN? – yessir,
it's 1975, the shah's
in place, the southeaster blows,
there're gulls in the sky,
two cable cars are halfway
up or down (respectively) and
outside the Cultural Museum
an old hunchback tries
to flog me 10c worth of unshelled

nuts. He's been here
since I was 15
trying to be Baudelaire, I'd maunder
round town watching women's legs, but now
I've only
eyes for postboxes and
my heart's in my packet: it's one thousand
illegal pamphlets to be mailed.

In blue bluer-than-any-sea doeks, in rubber galoshes,
Arm over arm, three lunch-time pals,
Three dark women and their laughter

As opposite the cannery my train arrives
From many years back and
Slows into Woodstock station.

Three women eating lunch, glimpsed
From the window.
Salt light for laughter, galoshes
Studded with a cat's
Eyed blink in a myriad of pellicles.

Three women, six knowing hands
Fresh from, x the number,
Bodies of fishes.
In gutting and scaling there being, I'd guess,
No malice, nor any your equals.

Your hands planing cross-grain to the flesh,
Your galoshes collecting the soft milt
Spray of hake scales.
Into your tender propitious hands, sisters,
From the night parts of the seas, I commend
Lucky – all fishes.

ONE PARTICULAR DAY. 1975

The municipal bins stood
stock still at dawn on that day
strapped to their individual poles
                    present
                present
            present
they intone in my mind's ear
if only to confirm by the simplest
roll call of their names:
Vullis Blik – *Hou U Stad* – *Keep Your City* –
Clean – that this place was real, ditto –
the sound of metal to metal from the cargo
ships hove to, close by in the bay
and the freight train's ring-ting-ting
memento loitering in a place long since
it has left behind – yes,
yes, all this occurred
with the sky's opening up
between the even now of things past
and the not yet where
already the footstep
of what's to come sounds.
At dawn of that day, downtown
an elevator marked *Goods & Non-Whites* began
slowly to rise, by the bus queue,
at the place of work, something
like viva mpla was whispered
through the wind-placarded mesh.
And from Paarden Eiland a tick bird cut
north – true as bob, hopes
high, head down, flying
                – feet crossed

A NAMING OF MATCHES

If you twirl a match
in your fingers, it'll
purr like cat:
This one, *Hothead.*
This one, *Firebird.*
This one's tipped with sorrow,
      – *Black Tear.*
This one, *Brazier Warmth.*
This one, *Primus Stove.*
Matches are
      . . . well, straightforward,
you can feel
in the palm of a hand
their honest weight, you can sense
the yellow flower
wrapped in each dark bud . . .
Strike, Ardent, Toothpick, Piper.
Row upon row in closed ranks they wait
for their baptism of fire.
      This one, *Single.*
      This one, *Spark.*
      This one,
            Prairie Fire.

LULLABY

But who killed Johannes, mama . . . ?
Ssssssssshhh! now close your eyes.
    Mama . . . ?
Only a bar of soap, they said.
So *thula, thula,* now quiet my child.

    But who killed Solomon, mama . . . ?
Ssssssssshhh! your blanket's tucked in.
    Who?
Only a length of rope, I suppose.
So *thula, thula,* now quiet my child.

    But who killed Ahmed, mama . . . ?
Ssssssssshhh! we must get up early.
    Please?
Only the tenth floor, I heard.
So *thula, thula,* now quiet my child.

    But who killed Steve, mama . . . ?
Ssssssssshhh! it's a long walk to the bus.
    Mama . . . ?
A brick wall, the magistrate said.
So *thula, thula,* now quiet my child.

    But who killed Looksmart, mama . . . ?
Ssssssssshhh! sleep and grow strong.
    Who, mama . . . ?
His own belt, that's what was blamed.
So *thula, thula,* now quiet my child.

    But who . . .
Thula! Thula! Thula! my child.

A TALE OF WHY TORTOISE CARRIES A HUT UPON HIS BACK

Once long ago, Tortoise challenged a large beast, saying:
    Why do you walk around in this veld
    as if it all belonged
    exclusively to you?

And the beast replied:
    Because I am huge,
    because I am great,
    because I am called
    Tyrannosaurus,
    because I have six-inch teeth
    I'm destined
    for a special, civilising role in this place.

But (just in case)
he made
Tortoise a prisoner and forced him to work
all day, every day, in a field.
Only late afternoons was Tortoise led back
to rest in the quietness of his cell.

Yet often on return he would find
the small world he'd made smashed,
his few books and letters scattered and awry,
and Tortoise felt anger in his throat
like some, half-swallowed
prehistoric stone.
The bed he'd made was ripped up,
his once folded clothes were scattered on the floor.
The beast had paid yet another visit
while Tortoise was away.

They say Tortoise is a patient one, yes,
he learnt to be by picking up the fragments of a shattered world
time and time again.
So that's why Tortoise took to carrying
his hut upon his back.
That was long ago.

They tell me Tyrannosaurus is now
extinct,
while Tortoise is alive and well, but you can still see
how he had to stick together broken pieces
– he's got marks on his shell.

CHAMELEON

In your cosmic repose
only the scandal
of two rolling planets betrays your avid
flypaper soul.
Wrapped in technicolour, worked
by fastidious
shifting-spanner toes,
each foot is
lifted slowly
one by
one by one, painstaking
on the track
of flies.

Pinnacle-back, confuser of nature's
metaphysical divides
on the ground evoking
your volcanic beginnings
you become
a stone among stones.
Or you climb up
into the arms of a tree and the tree
blushes
it thinks it has grown a strange
insectivorous leaf.
Last of the fire-breathers,
tongue-in-cheek dragon with your secret
mouthful of rolled-up pink
I have seen you
finally old with age
tiptoe to the end
turn a deep brown and wear
your own death
like another disguise.

KWIKKIE

Pernickety one
. . . quick-step
. . . penny-whistle walk
I like your style
fossicker
pointillist of our yard.
I've studied
your ratchet-work
your seamstress ways
stitch and pulley
I have thought myself
into the flywheel of your clockwork head.
I've watched you long
I know how it feels
to have eyes at the side, or
to end with a beak.

They call me
wagtail now
but actually
      I am cocking my head.

CLOTHES

Shoulder to shoulder with my shirt
I used to move around
Mostly in step with my pants.
We were almost inseparable, once,
Who would have guessed?

First they took my belt away,
Wrist watch, small change,
Later the rest, handed in a packet
To my visitors for safekeeping, and confined

To the same family wardrobe where
I'd hide away as a child, amongst the hush,
Mothballed shoes, cuffs, legs,
Arms, amongst my solemn
Ancestral ranks with their wire
Question marks for heads.

Inside and shutting the door, I'd go to find
How in my supposed absence – ssssh,
The world would sound,

In there. Resolves hardening in the same
Far away darkness, hanging on unrepentant, it's you now
Listening, you my clothes
Set to confound all our enemies,
Twenty more months now then
We pick up
Where we left off last.

SECOND THOUGHTS

My brother comes on a visit.
The shirt he's wearing looks
Very familiar indeed. The little
Upstart bastard . . . will I really
Ever get back to my clothes?
Or at least, is he who returns
Likely to be remotely the same?
A bit cranky perhaps stronger
Broken down more determined –
All of these things are
At least possibilities, you can't
Mothball yourself. Even in here.
And . . . ?
Okay. Life goes on.
My clothes should be worn.

Even the Dead

Even the Dead

Explaining Some Things

THREE REASONS FOR A MIXED, UMRABULO, ROUND-THE-CORNER POETRY

i.
A poem is meant to stand upon its own
Like a Grecian urn in some colonial museum,
The object of a contemplation
(Thou still unravish'd bride ...) that obscures:

The mud of its production;

The complicity in our gaze.

ii.
Between, let's say, May 1984 and May 1986
(Speaking from my own limited, personal experience,
    of course)
There was a shift out there
From lyric to epic.

iii.
Our contemporary, the great northern Ireland poet,
Writes from within and for
A culture that assumes Homer, Spenser, Yeats.

I live in a country with eleven official languages,
Mass illiteracy, and a shaky memory.

Here it is safe to assume
Nothing at all. **Niks.**

It's two days after the worst. We've just returned from
Johannesburg. We drop comrades in the vicinity, and decide, as
Trevor puts it, to have a look.

Along roads pitted with the remains of barricades, swerving and
bumping we go, eyes unpeeled.

Mahobe Drive has become a patrol strip. Armoured personnel
carriers move up and down its half kilometre. They ignore us.
Or, perhaps, they are watching closely. The hooded, slit-
windowed faces of the vehicles make us uncertain. We don't
linger.

Mahobe Drive is the cut-line, beyond it: ash and buckled zinc as
far as the eye sees. 80 dead, I have read. 2 000 shacks
destroyed. 20 000 homeless. Dull numbers to guess three days
of devastation that have just happened here.

In those three days the apartheid police and army have
destroyed an entire shanty-town, unleashing black vigilantes
(*witdoeke*), victims themselves turned perpetrators, to perform
much of the dirty work.

After-shocks, neuralgic points, are all around us now. An old
man stumbles along with a corrugated sheet of zinc on his back.
His eyes are blank with terror. He is half running, but from
whom, and to where?

Over by the church, which will itself be burnt down in the
coming days, there is a milling of refugees. People are jumpy.
Suddenly from their skittish midst a sprinting of three, twenty,
some sixty youth hurl themselves off in a wheeling pursuit. Or
are they fleeing?

We shouldn't, shouldn't be here.

Around the corner are the New Crossroads homes, formal
structures, the last line of sanctioned black poverty before

ground zero, the burnt-out acres of the shanty-town.

As we turn the corner, we see people in their front yards watching a strip of empty veld. There is a corpse lying there.

It moves. One knee bends and keels over.

Across the field, a young man draped in a blanket approaches the body. Casually he places sticks on its chest. Another figure strolls up to dowse the body with petrol.

All of this is done unhurriedly. In broad daylight. In the middle of an open field, before some hundred people, and around the corner from the police and army.

The lackadaisical visibility of this execution is, must be, the main point.

The executioners preparing the victim move back and forth, leaving him untended for many minutes at a time. This is ritual. A macabre human sacrifice on the lip of a still smouldering volcano, as if to stake challenge to its monopoly on death.

The car tyre, that will burn and burn, immolating the victim in its rubbery inferno, is now being rolled out and placed on his chest.

Let's go! Please! I am pleading with Trevor. The words I have been reciting finally spilling out.

But is it horror? Or rage at our own impotence? Or the self-disgust of the voyeur? Or is it fear that, while we watch, we too will be engulfed from behind, overpowered, knocked down and carried off by the police, or the youth, or the *witdoeke*?

But now the executioners themselves are disappearing, not running, not diminishing their authority, just melting away. The hundred-odd observers in the front yards of their homes are also fading off.

And just as suddenly the corpse in the middle of the field is up, and sprinting away. In our direction. A wild, hobbling dash.

The victory of life over death? Of the innocent small person caught in the middle?

But what is the middle?

Are you sure, in the thick of all this slaughter, he could be innocent?

Whom did he just betray? Whom will he still betray now as he runs away from the executioners?

Away from the spectators. Away from the police and army with fresh killings on their hands. A corpse covered in petrol, each stumbling pace one step more away from a death it has already died.

He is running towards us. Into our exile. Into the return of exiles. Running towards the negotiated settlement. Towards the democratic elections. He is running sore, into the new South Africa. Into our rainbow nation, in desperation, one shoe on, one shoe off. Into our midst. Running.

(1986–97)

Moorage

'without tenderness, it is hell'

Adrienne Rich

MOORAGE

i.
In its own armpit, a duck drops asleep
In the wind that rootles
In thorn scrub, *duiwel se grraan*
In Jorrie Barsby's brayed words.

Seventy-year old, *visterman*,
Lifelong inhabitant of this shore.
'Were you born here?' I ask.
'No,' he replies. 'You see
That house down the road?
I was born *there*.'

Which makes distance relative,
As is time for the fish of a tree
Planted, says Barsby, as
'Shade for my old age', on this
Sparse shore where trees do not
Easily grow, and those that manage
Are soon eaten down by cows.

Which is why, years off from any shade,
Jorrie Barsby's hope
Struggles towards old age
Knee high inside of its cow proof
Fish-net cage.

ii.
To live close to every tree you had ever planted.

Our century has been the great destructor of that,
The small and continuous community, lived in solidarity
With seasons, its life eked out around
Your fore-mothers' and -fathers' burial-ground.

iii.
Where the graveyard tilts up
For the headstones to see, stone brows
Of the dead to watch
Eastward across their lagoon.

Cornelius ('Sakkie') Petersen
Is there
Inscribed among them:

> *He was a Man*
> *Who would Give*
> *His last Fish*
>   *RIP*

From beside the church with its miracle
Of one palm, above the lagoon
Engraved as Galilee on the Sunday
Mind's eye of the fisherfolk, dead and alive

Along this actual shore from where
Cornelius Petersen has long since
Landed, scaled, given the ultimate
Fish away.

iv.
We call 'nature' something,
Frail as we know it, too, to be,
(A punctured ozone over ravished landscapes),
Something, nonetheless, more permanent,
Cyclical, more anchored, anchoring us,
The world in our minds, our minds in our bodies,
Our bodies in the world – something like this.

Nature: once touchstone of truth for the romantics.

For the modernisers: more, an untamed invitation.

For us: A weekend away in the midst of another
State of emergency.

v.
A banner? – No, you say,
It's the whole lagoon
That flaps out sunset-time
From their merest ankles.
Elbows, dipped, stilt, dipped,
Knee, through the shallows
Flamingoes push their slow
Collective scaffold.

'Nature?' – we wonder,
What does that mean?
Of this place,
'It's too good to be true,' you say
As we walk the beach.

We have come to reflect
On struggles in places
We have left behind
And end up speaking
Mostly of here and things

Where, listen, below
The fiscal shrike's
Squelchy-boot call it's
So quiet you can hear
The small craft
Puppy-keen, straining at moorage
Each with its own wet
Chop-licking side slaps.

When, along the beach, a dark

Woman, like an apparition, it's true,

Emerges, she asks, earnestly,

Hoping, I guess, against hope

Two older companions, women, laughing behind her,

She asks: Excuse me, we were arguing,

It's too good to be true, they say.

So are you:

Illicit lovers, newlyweds, or on a weekend fling?

vi.
Ask the stream of conscience
That feeds the lagoon.
For conscience is no puritan,
It is hope, sweet water

Rinsed, wrung, spilling,
Water gargled through rock,
Than a frog puddle growing
Both more now, and
                    Quieter.

Clear-eyed enough for the sky
To swallow this stolen
Glimpse of itself,
Ringed with palmiet,
Hidden in a tumble of rocks

Stay true, true, being
The hardest of struggles, stay true to your hopes,
Where the pool drops asleep
On a blink.

vii.
Or perhaps answers lie, blazon-wise,
In the item by item celebration of desire?
But not with the poet's gaze travelling over
A Grecian urn displayed in an imperial museum,
A plundered object for contemplation, nostalgia, or regret.
Not the female form alone, but
Our bodies, equal, vulnerable, conjugal, as in:

Entwined, nudged from under the tent's flap,
Our toes, before which, into air, clicking with static,
Tiny grasshoppers spring
Nitpicking, fine-comb's teeth.

As in: your eyes, stone green, going
Squigged up
When you laugh.

As in, ribbed
Are a sand-dune untouched;
A slip-way; to your tongue
The roof of my mouth.

As for the two round
Apples of your bum –
I think of the words of Oscar Mpetha
Spoken of other matters, and for another occasion,
– Comrades, he said, things start at the front, but
Everything must come from behind.

viii.
Fact: native North Americans fashion small nets
With feathers and shells
Which they suspend to trawl over sleepers:
To restrain nightmares and to glean,
From physical space, symbolic meanings.

ix.
Facing aft, then,
Back to deep waters,
Rowing like hell to get
The trek-net in place,
The spotter high on hill
Flag and whistle
Sends me out,
Pursuing an elusive
Darting of a shoal desired
That only I can catch

But only he can see.
And you are the one
Ankle deep in sand
Who holds to basic truths
Like the rope
Of the net's beginning.

Between the spotter
And yourself
Oarwood chafed in rowlocks
Here I am.
You insist on back.
The spotter waves me on.

x.
Gulled to disputation
Into every footprint we press
Some anger,
Into the headwind,
As we track in confusion, along the beach
Our separate, together, unreconciled ways,
Embroiled in our wrangles,
Our ravelling unpeelings,
Over the bones of us,
Over the pickings.
– God let us hold
Some certainty, our gull's hearts
Cry out – Enough.
Enough – raucously. Swivel-bodied, scavenger,
Skew on into the wind,
Or let us fall
Falling away
As suddenly, wind with the wind to within
One swoop of a
Centimetre
Over the hummocky sand.

xi.
Chock full,
With hidden motive
Is the rock pool.

Where under the lash of wave, overspilling,
Hard-case, recidivists, the barnacles
Knuckle down.

But closing, oh, its eyes with each,
To make a clean breast of it, with each
Wave the beach sighs: Kiss my belly, kiss ...

And everything about the way the whelk walks proclaims
Though the shell be firm
The flesh is willing.

xii.
So what are we attempting in this inter-tidal place
Of infatuation, erotic love, comradeship, quarrelling,
        companionship, back to infatuation again, or
All the way down to some future low water mark of
For the sake of the kids?

Is it the improbable notion to anchor
At the anchorage of carnal love,
Between two consenting adults,
A social scaffold called: family?
This entity of cooking, shopping, paying of bills,
Reproduction, the joint dodging of security police, and the
        rearing of kids?

For the record,
Without irony nor sense of moralising,
This IS the notion
We are attempting to live.
A small community at a biological moorage,
Or, I suspect you'd insist, the other way around.
Either way. Either way it is tenuous
Till death, and perhaps even beyond it,
Do us part.

xiii.
Because the struggle we haven't, in fact,
Left behind, as it flaps out
As this banner
Is also a struggle to make
The too good to be true be true.

Isn't it? Hmmm? We ask
In our hearts, thumping
Like small craft, puppy-keen
As we walk in our bodies.

Our biological moorage
To birth, love, death, that we push
In time always, and yet
Through all human times, stretched out
From toe to lip,
Like conjugal bodies
Affirming, something, moving now towards
Unabashed romantic closure,
Lagoon and land lie alive to and
Touching each other every
Inch of the way.

MAY DAY 1984

Epping Industrial, in your empty field by Langa station,

In your Cape Flats sands, by those four well-trod paths that
move towards work

Security arc-lights dim down now in the ground-hugging mist

At 6.30, on this, rainy autumn morning, it is, and still dark.

Along the paths, for those in whose tread and march, my theory
says, the future lies,

Moving in huddles which become 2, 3, 5 separate individuals
only when less than ten feet off, as they pass,

Grabbing indifferent, or friendly, with a nod of recognition or a
silent get stuffed.

I'm handing out a pamphlet, unbelongingly, longingly, 'Let us
win May Day as a public holiday!' it says,

As an old man comes by, with a limp and a slouch.

Another, head recessed into coat collar, has, down his pipe-
bowl, this thumb, tucked in fast.

Three women walk quickly, making sleepy laughter from inside
of there, I mean, beneath their collective hood.

A youngster, dreadlocks a-bob, runs to beat the clock.

Whoaa, hokaai! I want to say. No,

Run on, wheel in the day, make laughter, limp, limp, limp on, ta, ta,

May your thumb

Hold the warmth.

YOU-DEE-EFF

There was a new English in the air
As mass-based organisations sprang up
And nouns turned into verbs.
'We haven't **caucused** it yet', 'Who's **chairing?**',
'We must **workshop** this thing.'
There was a rush of acronyms:
AZASO, COSAS, GWU, CUSA, MACWUSA.
Talk of Gee-Cee's and R-Ee-Cee's,
And of Ank and Ukkas.
Syllabised words grew from initials,
Essay, the country we lived in, Sudef,
The soldiers who, one and a half years on,
Would begin to invade townships,
Door to door in pursuit
Of agitators lurking behind acronyms.
Still, Oo-Whoah remained U, double U, O:
The United Women's Organisation,
And the family circle extended, older women,
Some national figures, others grass-roots cadres,
Were known, African custom-wise, as Ma,
Or Mama (Ma Sisulu, Mama Dora),
Or Auntie (**Ooh, daai auntie kan vloek**)
When they organised on the Cape Flats.
An abbreviated **com**, for comrade, travelled
National, tongue to tongue, a small badge
Even in the most desolate, racially downtrodden
Townships of the platteland. 'Ja, com,'
People were saying, everywhere, as they shifted
The stress down to the very last syllable,
'We must orga-NISE.'

MAY DAY 1986

In the white suburbs, where I live, it is like a purloined Sunday, quiet, and with minimal traffic. But out in Bellville South, in the civic hall there is bustle. Preparations are under way for one of four trade union rallies in the Cape Town region. I'm out there with Gemma, my wife, a union full-timer. The rally is due to start in three hours.

Tchee-weep-tock-tock. The sound system is going through its testing ... One-two ... one-two ... testing. Banners are being hoisted up on walls. 'More to the right. No man, the RIGHT, ek sê!' Over there, a group of marshals is briefed. 'I want you guys to get your arses into gear. Only two accredited journalists and one photographer will be allowed in, get it?'

Now it's one hour to go. Are people coming? This is always a nervous moment for the organisers. There is news ('Man, the cops come') that the system is blocking people on their way to the meeting. 'They were driving the vans like anything. They chased us in the vans.'

At Serepta and Bellville train stations, the two nearest to the venue, workers are being forced back on to trains by the police. We also hear that workers from the Brackenfell hostels were teargassed and dispersed in the township on their way to the buses. 'The government, why she do this thing?' Two union organisers and three workers have been arrested. 'Last week it was worse. This week it will be worse, worse.'

But the hall fills up, spilling over beyond its capacity by 2.00 pm. There are songs and speeches. One group of Brackenfell workers, who have managed after all to evade the police cordon, march in, a half-hour late, singing and with banners. More speeches. More songs.

The chairperson is enthusiastic, but unaccustomed to controlling mass rallies. 'Workers and residents of Cape Town, by which I mean all of you, children of Africa ... Please, comrades, please, can I have some silence', he shouts hopelessly above the singing. He clearly doesn't know the syntactic markers of a rally. Zenzo, the interpreter, moves up to assist. 'Amaaaa-ndla!', he calls, and immediately the whole hall stops short in its singing to reply: 'A-wee-thu!'

The chairperson can proceed. 'Thank you, comrades, our next speaker is …'

At the end, after the singing of the national anthem, and the shouting of five amandlas, five viva COSATUs, the meeting closes.

Outside the hall many of the buses for the workers from the hostels have not arrived. They've been sent back, as we later realise, by the police. On the road outside, at either end of the block, are two police Casspirs, armoured personnel carriers.

Most of the several thousand from the meeting safely leave on foot for the stations, or for the surrounding ghetto. But some hundreds of workers are stranded without buses. We mill around with them outside the hall waiting for transport. One of the police Casspirs edges forward. A metallic voice from the belly of the armoured vehicle is saying something: 'Klug – wah-wah. Klug – wah-wah.'

What?

The message is repeated, eventually becoming clearer – 'YOU HAVE THREE MINUTES TO DISPERSE!'

Suddenly there is a gun-shot, **Blam!** And another, **Blam!** People edge back against the outer wall of the hall. The gun-shots turn out to be two teargas cylinders fired a little short of us, and now streaming away 40 metres off.

A delegation of three, including Gemma, moves up to the Casspir. We watch nervously. Three small figures approach the faceless, metal beast. A short exchange occurs. We can feel how their necks must be prickling now with each step, as they return, backs to an armoured vehicle laden with trigger-happy police.

'The cops said they have nothing to say to us. They've ordered us back into the hall.'

People start moving back.

Suddenly – **Blam! Blam! Blam! Blam!** A volley of shots. For a paralysing moment you don't know if it is teargas, rubber bullets or hard ammunition.

It's teargas again, this time dozens of canisters right into our midst. Still more are fired, **Blam! Blam! Blam! Blam!** There is a surging, panicky push into the hall. I'm left, stuck outside. I shelter behind a side wall, out of sight from where I imagine the Casspir now finds itself. But I have badly judged where to hide. I am taking in large amounts of teargas.

Since last year they have changed its chemical composition. The people of the townships became adept at dousing themselves in water to neutralise the effects of the gas. In the big political marches and funerals last year, all along the route, township dwellers would place buckets of water, as an expression of solidarity and as a precaution. Standard gear for the young lions, the youthful activists, became a water-soaked scarf.

But this year the gas is activated by damp. It burns the moist membrane of your nostrils. It eats away at your throat. Your eyes water and that triggers more vicious stinging. You are blinded. Your nervous system short circuits, a momentary paralysis sets in. And now the stomach heaves, retching up emptiness.

Out of the mist I see a darting figure. A young kid. 'Come, com ...,' he grabs my hand, and we crouch-run for some thirty metres. 'Through here, through here,' he pushes me through a hole in the vibracrete wall around the civic hall. On the far side he asks, 'You okay, com?' I nod, feeling grateful and a little bashful at being rescued by a kid no more than ten years of age.

The run has made my stomach feel better, although my eyes are weeping, and the tears keep reactivating the gas.

I find myself in the company of four streetwise, working-class kids from the neighbourhood. They take it upon themselves to escort me around. They know every wall hole and scalable fence. They know which side of a lane, being less visible, is safer. They operate like a small platoon, one scouting ahead, one watching the rear. We move across a school ground, sprinting between trees. We flatten ourselves down the side of a prefab block of class-rooms. The leader of the group squats down, getting his eyes to knee level, below the foliage-line of the surrounding scrubs.

'Daar! Daar kom hulle. Don't run, come this way.'

This evading but staying in touch goes on for some 40 minutes.

I'm anxious that the comrades in the hall might be concerned about me.

It turns out that I am one of the lucky ones. The few hundreds who got back into the hall, were then shut in. Volleys of teargas were fired into the hall, and then gas-masked police charged in with quirts, viciously whipping choking people, young and old, men and women. Gemma has three large, bleeding weals across her thighs.

* * * * * *

That was our May Day 1986. A small episode in a countrywide action that turned out to be the biggest, to that date, political strike in our country's history. The people had proclaimed their own public holiday. Some two and a half million workers and students were involved.

The next day in their editorials, the newspapers congratulate the authorities for showing a more than customary restraint.

THE MIRACLE OF FISHES

You said:
It's the fault of a handful of agitators.

The agitators said (they liked to quote Mao):
We are fishes.

Meaning, in a sea that was us,
The great majority, the excluded-included.

Settled, unsettled, resettled beyond your horizons,
Beyond the rail-tracks and the ring of free-ways.

Far enough, but close enough,
To be labourers, domestic workers, Pep Store consumers.

Scattered, but crammed together,
Dispersed from your power centres,
We were regimented and encircled.

So we turned these exclusions
Into places of empowerment.
The township, the bush college, even the prison yard
Became
School for cadres.

Of us, you said: They are foreigners.

But still you solicited our custom.
Daily you wheeled us
Through the portals of the city.
We were Greeks,
You supplied the wooden horses.

For a day, or days, or weeks
We rejected these third class inclusions.
We declared stayaway.
We boycotted buses, shops, dummy elections.

We demanded a real say, but always you declined.
So we turned micro-space into parliament.

Umrabulo ruled in the street committee,
Debate raged through SRCs, and church halls,
Even the burial ground became
Lekgotla.

You called this communism
(You were more profound than any of us realised).

You called it:
        Total Onslaught.
You unleashed:
        Total Strategy.

The violence which had always
Pressed down upon us
Now came in through the windows
        Of our township trains,
        Of the very rooms where we slept and held vigil.

You recruited pseudo Greeks,
Green Beans, Black Cats, Witdoeke, Askaris.
These were infiltrated into the bellies
Of the wooden horses.
Cynically you called the result
Black on black violence.

In this way you applied
The Pentagon maxim:
If you can't catch the fish, poison the waters.

But still, still we resisted.

What began when you said
It's just a handful of agitators,

Ended in this:
We, the great majority, the excluded-included became
30 million local councillors,
30 million parliamentarians,
30 million agitators.

        The miracle of the multiplication of fishes.

POEM IN A SMALL FIST
(for G and B)

Erasing distance
Between the pleasure and its sign
At the breast our newborn enacts
The utmost beginning of every
Lyrical poem in his fist

That clasps and unclasps
As it floats along
With its cattail's wisp
And his whole snuffling soul weighs down
Into his lipples

But above
Is his fist
As closest to not being after as could be as any
Rippling
After-trace on pleasure.

＊＊＊＊＊＊

Tracked and wanted
On the run for two years
My mug shot
On their charge-office walls

In the depths of their emergency
Benjy's fist
Is this flag

Our own in its way
Raised up to say
This is a people's war.

We shall wage it
As people.

(Cape Town, mid-1987)

114

ON WATCH

i.

Home, almost it could be, home,
As the frog's call runs a small finger
Up and down, grook-grick-grook,
Tonight's gap-toothed comb.

The dirty war has receded, for the moment,
Unlikely, so I reckon, they will come
As a raiding party, gung-ho, this night,
Faces blackened and dark bandanas,
Dead of night, or later, if airborne,
Chopper blades churning first light.

All of this, which has happened
Here and hereabouts before,
Is unlikely tonight. Nonetheless,
Pen in hand, poem on page,
At my feet a Kalashnikov – broad
Strategic calculations notwithstanding.

Grook-grick-grook, and then
Dawn. And zick. The lights go down,
Stars slink off, same with the moon
Leaving behind its one pale, bloep,
Thumbprint, stuck to the sky.

ii.

Christ is the Answer is the banner
Corner Kwacha Road. The question
Is less obvious. Unless it be the 'Rock of Ages'
Minibus that teeters round
The self-same corner with its too many,
My own uncertainties, hanging on,
Like an abnormal load.

Exile means this. Not knowing
The question, nor getting beyond
The surface of Lusaka's dusty signs, this one
Proclaims: **Ministry of Decentralisation. HEADQUARTERS.**

Or the child's kite above the squatter camp.
Patched from a thrown-away plastic bag,
Yearning at a string, between
This sky and this Fourth World.

I'm sick of exile, says Themba Miya.
I want to be home, where I can
Catch hell (and throw some).

(ANC IPC House, Lusaka – mid-January 1990)

AND WHAT'S BECOME OF?
(for K and F)

... And so and so?
It's the last night of her stay,
So we reach into our lives,
Our way of affirming
Faith to each other,
Touching the discontinuous
That only we now seem
To hold together
In this what's become of?
Those we knew together,
Who have gone off
Into other lives.
Or who've simply
Gone. Like her husband, who I hear
For the first time now
Was dying for two years, and he knew it,
And she knew it, and I didn't, which casts
A whole different light
Upon my sunny eighth and ninth
Years upon this earth
Just as my five-days-old daughter's birth
The reason for my mother's flying visit
(Which is coming to an end this night)
Casts, upon all those that only we now
Hold together in this last night's recollecting,
Casts her only-just, her flickering,
Five-days-old life's sacred light.

(Johannesburg, July 1991)

THIS CITY

Joburg's high summer packs tall clouds aloft
As we drift into never-never,
Windows uptight, door-knobs down.

It's Mozart, commuting through the littered streets,
On my car stereo, through this unlovely town.
The heart torn out, suburbed, scattered, shopping-malled,
And beyond are the dark moons:
Alexandra, Thembisa, Vosloo, Soweto.

I live in the inner suburbs where
Endangered, the panting lupus, *pasop vir*,
Has long since staged a domestic return,

And our own privatised armed responders,
The very ones, perhaps, whose coming
In Lusaka once I feared, are now
A mere touch-pad in our night away.

This is a screwed-up, wounded city, bruised
By the abusings of its past,
Stoop-shouldered, hard-talking, vulgar,
Gauteng's (you have to hawk to say that) epicentre,
One of the one hundred big cities of the globe.

To live in this unchosen place is to choose
A city among cities, like a Seoul or Sao Paulo,
Where, despite it all, the working people
Still possess capacity and motivation
To shake and shake and shake the coming age.

Here we live. Here, where without
Compassion, comradeship, tenderness
        It is hell.

(Johannesburg 1997)

Even the Dead

JOE SLOVO'S FAVOURITE JOKE

'It's Cuba, you know, 1959. The guerrilla forces have just taken power, and there is a hurried meeting of the leadership in the newly liberated Havana. Afterwards, shaking his head, a bewildered Che Guevara takes his friend aside: 'Comrade Fidel, why on earth have you made me Minister of Banking?'

'Well, you put up your hand when I asked: Who here is an economist?'

'Oh my no-o-o,' groans Che. 'I thought you asked: Who here's a COMMUNIST?'

* * * * * *

The struggle calls for more than laughter.
But also laughter. History can advance on its funny side
By freak, frailty and unplanned – Joe understood that.

As he understood the imperative of the plan,
Decisive action, the general line, which is why

In the last years of his life, it wasn't the collapse
Of the wall of stone certainty alone,
But something deep in his personality

That led him to recommend both
Socialism and the market.

I imagine now him saying: The plan
Is the plan, and the market
         Is a joke.

Under capitalism – a bad joke.
Under socialism ...
who knows?

FIVE THOUGHTS CONCERNING THE QUESTION: 'WHAT HAPPENS AFTER MANDELA GOES?'

1   With the words 'after' and 'goes'
    The question at least proves
    We are not living in a theocratic dynasty like, say,
    North Korea's.

2   He stands on an ancient threshold.
    One foot in the commune, one foot
    In a once barely emergent aristocracy.
    No easy walk.
    And so he walks, stolid, uneasily-easily,
    Through this cynical end of the 20th century,

    Ranging the globe with arcane values:
    Of honour, pride, stubbornness, dignity
    And a tradition of leadership to be earned
    Only in daily communion with a people.

3   Something like all of this could get lost
    After Mandela goes.

4   From an organisational viewpoint,
    'What after?' betrays another anxiety.

    'There is only one-one-ONE ANC,' I've been told.
    I agree, provided
    The next question isn't:

    Whose?

5   For the sake of democracy
    These words should be thoroughly mistrusted:
    'Identity'; 'we have always', and 'in the image of'.

    Not to mention:
    'Crown prince'.

POEM FOR MANDELA

It's impossible to make small-talk with an icon
Which is why, to find my tongue,
I stare down at those crunched-up,
One-time boxer's knuckles.

In their flattened pudginess I find
Something partly reassuring,
Something slightly troubling,
Something, at least, not transcendent.

A REPLY TO PABLO NERUDA

It is true, Lautaro
Survived cascades, thorns, crags,
Slept under the sheets of snowdrifts, and
Emerged from his trials a formidable hero.

But it was only then
The Araucanian chieftain's
Fuller education began.

He had to compel himself now

To train his ear in the tree of sympathy,
To draw knowledge from small pots,
To acknowledge his debt to those many years younger.

A fearless campaigner,
A sjambok's blow in the face of injustice,
He had to learn now
The harder things

To respect the majority,
To habituate his feet to the ways of the people,
To acquire the humility in the hop of a sparrow.

He bathed himself, reluctant at first, in the waters of
    consultation,
He learned nothing can be won except by the masses.

He taught his heart to despise self-serving servitude to the
    people,
He instructed his tongue in the difference between we-simple
    (meaning us), and we-royal (meaning I).

He came to accept that this was more than a question of
    grammar.

He quarried in the mud pit of history,
He acknowledged that those hardened in struggle can end up
    with stone hearts.

He pitied the baobab.

He discovered a mandate is a weapon, not a limitation.
He sharpened his critical eye first in his own mirror.
He counselled others to mistrust claims, especially his own, to
     being infallible.

He grasped the dangers of speaking alone to the python.
He noted the guile of the enemy.
He stopped underestimating the alligator's intention.

Slowly, he accepted noble suffering was not enough.

He learnt everything remains impermanent.

He realised leadership is not enlightened patronage, nor the
     balancing of factions.

He took time to grasp that those most flattering to his own
     vanity, were those most unreliable.

In short,

Lautaro came to understand

Surviving trial by fire, exile, stone, limitless time, or steel bars is
     only the beginning of being

Worthy of the people.

THE TROUBLE WITH REVOLUTIONISM

We were so seized with revolution
We entirely forgot reform ...

Of family, work-place, bureaucracy, police force ...

Having abolished the bosses,
We became the bosses.

(In the name of the workers, of course.)

THE TROUBLE WITH REFORMISM

Politics is
Not the science of the probable,
Not the struggle for the desirable.

We scoffed at anything out of ordinary.

Politics, we said, is the art of the possible.
We are artists, and our craft:
        Embroidery.

THE TROUBLE WITH CERTAIN MARXISTS

Time passed on this earth as we debated
The ultimate step into socialism.
A generalised crisis? Elections? Insurrection?

We were experts on the final moment.
And time passed. And we debated.

EPITAPHS

For a Stalinist
Here lies an immortal brain
Long before death
It was a mausoleum

For a Finance Minister
Grounded, here lies our beloved minister
Propagator of the Passenger
Theory of Propulsion

He asked us to tighten belts
Not because of, but in order to

Take off

For an ultra-leftist
She lived each passing Year
In the Duty-Free Zone
Though
Always with Much to Declare

For the True Source
Of the Unnamed Source
Deeply Missed
Here
In Death as in Life
Lies
BRAZENLY

A Journalist

For a recently Departed
Soul from the new Patriotic Bourgeoisie
Hey, man, don't weep
I can't take your call presently
As I'm upwardly mobile

Please leave your prayer
After the beep

For the writer of Epitaphs
You who pass by now pause and ponder

Here lies
Jeremy Cronin

Who could possibly have wished this untimely death?
I wonder

THE TIME OF PROPHETS

*Through the first half of the 19th century, the Xhosa
peoples bore the brunt of a British colonial army of occupation.
For a people for whom war was, at most, cattle raiding, in
which the defeated were readily absorbed into one's own tribal
structure, the experience of total war was new, incomprehensible
and terrifying. Crops were laid waste; hundreds of square miles
of land seized; men, women and children annihilated. There was
nothing in the old beliefs to explain, let alone ward off this
catastrophe.*

*In May 1856, a young woman, Nongqawuse, went to draw
water at the Gxara stream. She met four young men. They were
the spirits of the dead, eternal enemies of the colonial settlers.
They had come from battle-fields beyond the seas to aid the
Xhosa people.*

*Nongqawuse's uncle, Mhlakaza carried the message to the
paramount chief, Kreli. The spirits had given orders that all cat-
tle, the great wealth of the Xhosa people, were to be killed
and that no-one was to cultivate the land. Then, on a certain
day, millions of fat cattle would spring out of the earth and
great fields of corn, ready for eating, would appear. At the same
time the sky would fall and crush the whites and with them all
those blacks who had not obeyed.*

*With the full support of Kreli, the cattle-killing began
almost immediately. There were believers and doubters, but the
ranks of the believers steadily swelled. According to a
contemporary European observer, writing a few months after the
start of the cattle-killing: 'I think not less than three or four
hundred thousand cattle have been killed or wasted.'*

*On the day designated for the miracle the sun rose in the
east. It reached high noon. In the evening, as Ifubesi the owl
stirred in his bush, the sun set behind a veil of mist in the west.
Nothing, nothing untoward had happened. Famine deepened in
the land.*

However, not everyone was a loser. The labour shortage in the white settler farms and towns of the Cape Colony was alleviated. There would be other armed struggles, but the early tribal resistance of the Xhosa peoples had now been irreparably shattered.

* * * * * *

These things had been heard in this land before

Midwives remembered the name Nongqawuse

Elders in the villages whispered of the cattle-killing

But our virtual-reality, modern-day soothsayers, living in global time, were oblivious

As they scanned the banking journals and followed the futures markets.

They sniffed out statistics and tut-tutted over our latest world-competitiveness ratings.

Each one had his or her own diagnostic

Yet everyone simply confirmed a consensus.

We had to send the right signals,

We had to appease the markets, a great sacrifice was required.

Every failure was attributed, in a frenzy of reproach, to conflicting signals, insufficient resoluteness, to the breaking of ranks.

Anthropologists objected.

This hysteria, they said, was the symptom of cultural stress.

This was a moment in which, old models having failed, one could fear a switch from secular to sacred.

The historians said this was a period of transition, a time in which there was danger leadership would pass to prophets, the Nxeles, firebrands, eclectics who talked in formulaic tongues, who brooked no contradiction, who opined with the arrogance of neophytes.

But these observations were brushed aside.

The diviners presented themselves not as high-priests, but as economists in communication with the mysteries of stock market sentiment.

The shade of Nongqawuse tried to speak out, a second time, now in warning, this time more soberly,

But neither she nor the midwives were consulted, the elders were ignored, the plight of the unemployed young bypassed, historians and anthropologists were scoffed at.

Despite moral intuition, commonsense and ancient wisdom, despite concrete evidence,

Despite great tragedies across our borders, the cosmology of the World Bank prevailed.

It was called belt-tightening, deregulation, shock therapy, wage restraint, privatisation, it was called becoming competitive, it was called a winning-nation formula.

The time of a new cattle-killing was at hand.

EVEN THE DEAD

Walter Benjamin:
'There is a secret agreement between past generations and the present one. Our coming was expected on earth. Like every generation that preceded us, we have been endowed with a form of Messianic power, a power to which the past has a claim. That claim cannot be settled cheaply.'

* * * * * *

Every week I read the back page of *Martin Creamer's Engineering News*, profiles of business leaders. Last week it was the turn of:

Full name: Joggie Heuser
Position: Chief Executive of Soekor
Date and place of birth: May 1938, Bloemfontein
Education: Kroonstad High, 1955; B Comm, Pretoria 1960
Value of assets under your control: More than R1-billion
Hope for the future: For all South Africans to bury the past unconditionally ...

* * * * * *

It's Johannesburg 1996. It's F W De Klerk. He's addressing a breakfast meeting of the American Chamber of Commerce.

It's in the same week of another week of the Eugene De Kock trial. Tortures, Third Force hit squads, mutilated bodies.

And it's the same story in the same week of another week of the Truth and Reconciliation Commission.

In this same week, then, De Klerk is telling the American Chamber of Commerce: 'Nowhere else in Africa will you find a country in which five large domestic banking conglomerates hold the savings of the population. In no other African country will you find such a developed insurance industry.'

And De Klerk smiles, the practised smile of the practised speaker, to signal joke coming up.

'People talk a lot about a Third Force,' De Klerk says with a twinkle in his eye. 'But in South Africa, the real Third Force is the private sector.' Unquote.

* * * * * *

That was in May.

In June, the *Financial Mail*, in its *Did You Hear* column, has another little joke – and I quote: 'Scheduled SABC2 coverage of the Truth Commission was dropped on Sunday and replaced with a programme called *Circus on TV*. Did anyone notice the difference?' (Snigger) Unquote.

These civilised sneers that allow themselves to slip out on the fun pages of the financial press, or at breakfast meetings, or up there on the 20th storey, in the corridors, where they feel safe and among themselves.

* * * * * *

I am not sure what poetry is. I am not sure what the aesthetic is. Perhaps the aesthetic should be defined in opposition to anaesthetic.

Art is the struggle to stay awake.

Which makes amnesia the true target and proper subject of poetry.

Amnesia, we are told, exists across two axes – the paradigmatic and the syntagmatic – as a similarity disorder, or as a contiguity disorder.

* * * * * *

Amnesia is when General Geldenhuys tells us the apartheid armies were never defeated at Cuito Cuanavale.

To prove his point, the general in his memoirs superimposes a diagram of a rugby field on to a map of southern Angola. Here is one set of poles, up here at Cuito. And here are the other poles, down here on a line that runs through Jamba, Sloma, all the way into Zambia.

With a rugby field tilted south-east like this it's clear, when
General Geldenhuys was pushed due south all the way down to
and over the Namibian border – that wasn't part of the game, it
was off the field.

The variant of amnesia is easily diagnosed in this case.

Severe paradigmatic amnesia.

The general believes it was rugby he was playing.

  * * * * * *

But it was golf, and it was amnesia,

When the Little Maestro, Gary Player, acknowledged his British
Open victory, saying South Africa's sporting achievements are
impressive indeed considering 'we only have three million
people'.

* * * * * *

It wasn't rugby.
  It was golf.
    And it isn't, above all,
  A whole new ball-game now

Because past dispossession still pays the dispossessor
  In compound interest

Apartheid still declares
  An annual dividend

Soekor retains R1-billion assets
  Whose origins have been buried
  Unconditionally

  * * * * * *

It's syntagmatic amnesia (container for contained) when the offi-
cial journal of my organisation, the African National Congress,
salutes the inauguration of President Mandela with a
cover, 'Free At Last!', and whoossssh, 6 Impala jets flying over
the Union Buildings. 'Free At Last!', it proclaims, forgetting to

133

ask – who pilots the planes?

It's amnesia when the SATV launches itself into the new South
Africa and lands
     In Las Vegas
          (Ongoing, chronic, paradigmatic amnesia)

Amnesia is the fate of the 46 who were killed in Johannesburg
     But not
          Outside of Shell House
     On the day of the so-called Shell House massacre

Amnesia declares a minister innocent of apartheid-era corruption
because she was
     Declared innocent by an apartheid-era commission

Amnesia appoints another commission, the Lethe Commission,
the Limbo Commission, Nirvana Commission, Justice van
deFerred Commission

Amnesia prevails when we claim we have returned to the family
of nations
     Forgetting to ask:
          Who is we?
     Forgetting to wonder:
          WHAT family?

Amnesia classifies Third World countries as 'developing'
     (structurally adjusted amnesia)

CNN is globalised amnesia

The Gulf War – lobotomised amnesia

Santa Barbara, the Bold and the Beautiful, Restless Years – the
milk of amnesia

Amnesia embraces the global reality of 23 million per annum
dead of hunger and hunger-related disease
That's a daily average equivalent, in fatalities, of one Hiroshima
     Buried each day

Under the cloud of amnesia

When Chris Hani was alive the newspapers described him as a
populist war-monger
When Chris Hani was assassinated the newspapers declared him
a man of peace
(pandemic, editorial amnesia)

There is upwardly mobile amnesia
        Affirmative action amnesia
                Black economic empowerment, the world owes
me one, Dr Motlana, give me a slice of it amnesia
        (syntagmatic amnesia – an elite for the whole)

There is winning-nation amnesia
        It puts in Olympic bids

        It summits Everest and forgets to name all but one
        Of the sherpas who carried us up

Winning-nation amnesia implies
        Some win, many lose

        And where does that leave Mozambique, Zimbabwe,
        Zambia, Angola, Lesotho and Swaziland?

        And where does that leave us
                In any sustainable future?

Beware, amnesia has no cut-off date

Beware, right now amnesia is sneering at us

Up there on the 20th floor, listen, over the cocktails, the
civilised sniggers on the pages of the *Financial Mail*

After all, we're a normal society now, except, perhaps, for the
unions and the violence

Apartheid was all the fault of those bearded chaps who like to
dress up in khaki uniforms

(I mean, who else benefited?)

No need to stand before Archbishop Tutu pleading forgiveness

Heavens no

After all, who needs AMNESTY

When there's

Blue-chip, just the ticket, deregulated, liberalised, privatised,
free market, god-given, just to please yer, property claused,
heck I worked for it all – I earned it, affirmative actioned – not
me, now in stock, just the product, your station, people of the
south, Felicia (what's my name again?), this one's for you

It's great, it's easier, I promise you, so let's hear it again from ...

Walter Benjamin:
    'In every era the attempt must be made anew to wrest
tradition away from a conformism that is about to overwhelm it
... Only that historian will have the gift of fanning some sparks
of hope in the past who is firmly convinced that even the dead
will not be safe from the enemy if he wins. And this enemy has
not ceased to be victorious.'